The Art Of Self-Compassion

a creative guide to being kind to yourself

Elizabeth McCarthy

Space Whale Productions
Presents: The Art of Self
Compassion - a creative
guide to being kind to yourself

First Edition

cover layout by Vix Volante Creative

cover artwork by Jen Watkins

Hand drawn + written by Elizabeth McCarthy,
the book features poetry by Eleanor Coffey
+ chapter illustrations by Jen Watkins.

ISBN: 9780648217701

May There Be Kindness In Your Gaze When You Look Within

— John O'Donohue

Contents

Sometimes My Love

Sometimes
my love for myself
looks like this

sitting quietly
anger rushes through me
like a train in the night
enough, it says
I see this nonsense
and that's enough

whatever you may think
your self is, as my self is

this self, needs love
needs defending, tending
through its numberless seasons

this self
sometimes a blazing newborn sun
or frost on a windshield

sometimes a cup overflowing with wine
or a dried up leaf

Sometimes a rolling log in the forest
or a thousand flying arrows

sometimes a sleeping cat in your bed
or smooth white bones on a sandy beach

but why love these things?
why love your own precious heart?

there is really no good reason
that I can think of

and yet
sitting quietly
I understand for myself
when to fight
and when to let it be
when to close
and when to open
when to say no
and when to say yes

and I know
that sometimes
this is just what it means
to live together
here, with my self.

introduction

I'M A BIG ^ BABY
WITTLE

I'VE REACHED (APPARENTLY) ADULT STATUS. BUT I STILL FEEL LIKE A WITTLE SCARED BABY

I made this book for all of us big babies out there trying to do adult life the best we can. I was inspired by researchers Kristen Neff + Chris Germer whose great work on self-compassion helped me realise its importance and profound benefits. I decided that I needed to actively practice self-compassion and integrate it into my daily life. The process of writing this book has given me ample opportunity to practice self-compassion in the face of all kinds of self criticism + judgement. I have long struggled with a harsh inner critic and a number of shame gremlins (particularly around creativity).

This book draws on mindfulness techniques (bringing our attention to the present moment), as well as art therapy activities. The intention is not to create amazing works of art (though that might happen) but to enjoy the process and be open to receiving insight and guidance into our lives.

Through exploring the creative process ~~that~~ we often find a window into ways of being that are not always easily accessible in our daily lives.

I hope this book will be a guide for you to explore the practice of self-compassion. I wish you well ♡ Liz

Practicing Self-Compassion

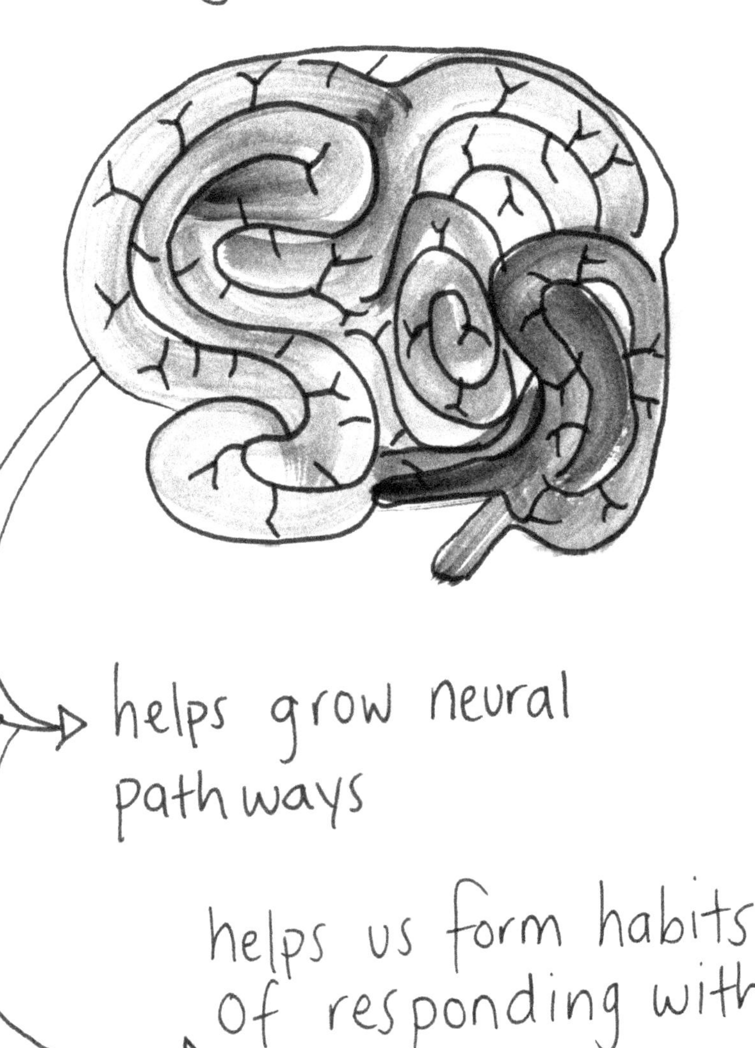

helps grow neural pathways

helps us form habits of responding with kindness

The self-compassion experts say that it's important that we respond to all of our pain with kindness.

even if it's a small thing like running late for an appointment

even if it's self-inflicted through our own actions

We can build our self-compassion pathways through choosing to respond to our suffering with kindness.

A Delicious feedback loop

OTHERS

compassion toward others can help boost our self-compassion

Self-compassion towards ourselves leads to more compassion toward others

SELF

THINGS THAT CAN GET IN THE WAY

I deserve to suffer!

Compassion is for the weak.

Maybe I'm just indulging my bad behaviour if I'm kind to myself.

I don't have time to be kind. It's a self-indulgent thing to do anyway.

I did this to myself and so I deserve to suffer

If I just beat myself up about this, I won't do it again.

You've got to be cruel to be kind.

GROW
HURRY
UP

WHY ARE
YOU NOT
A TREE
ALREADY

I CAN'T
EVEN LOOK
AT
YOU

WHAT HELPS WITH BEING KIND?

PRACTICING MINDFULNESS

Curiosity

What is this feeling?

Coming back to the present

Breathe in + out

What can I experience in this moment?

Gentleness

self-soothing words + touch

Awareness

noticing when I'm spiralling into self-criticism or shame

Space

allow difficult feelings to be there

meet + greet
- the child within

It can be difficult to be kind to ourselves. Something which can help is imagining ourselves as a child. In loving and caring for our inner child we can love and care for our adult selves.

Getting in touch with our inner child can also remind us of the things that bring us joy and help us feel alive.

We begin this chapter by remembering our inner child and returning to our own childhood for inspiration.

WHEN I WAS A KID I LIKED...

WHEN I WAS A KID I LIKED . . .

(think about your favourite activities, music, pets, colours, toys, outfits, games + stories)

DRAW OR WRITE

WRITE A STORY OR DRAW A PICTURE LIKE A KID.

I like green. I have green overalls. I like to climb trees and look over the fence to the neighbours. I have a dog called Oscar I like soccer and swimming. This is my family

BY ELIZABETH

WRITE AND DRAW YOUR STORY

WHAT THINGS FROM YOUR CHILDHOOD ARE STILL PART OF YOUR ADUIT LIFE?

WHICH THINGS FROM YOUR CHILDHOOD WOULD YOU LIKE TO EXPERIENCE OR EMBRACE MORE AS AN ADULT?

THE CHILD WITHIN

DRAW YOURSELF AS A CHILD.

BE KIND TO LITTLE

____________________ (insert your name)

Find or print a photo of Yourself as a child. Stick it here ↓

Take some time to look at the drawing or photo of you as a child.

What thoughts, emotions, memories or images arise?

Do you have anything to say to you as a child?

Does your child have anything to say to you?

Reflect. Write. Draw.

Reflect. Write. Draw.

HOLDING YOUR CHILD AND YOURSELF

- ♥ PUT YOUR HAND ON YOUR HEART
- ♥ BREATHE DEEPLY IN AND OUT
- ♥ TELL YOUR CHILD SELF WHAT IT NEEDS TO HERE

I love you.
You are safe.
You are free to play + enjoy.
You are very precious to me.

FREE PLAY

meet + greet
- the inner critic

INNER, INNER CRITIC. INNER CRITIC PRESSURE.

My critic gets loud when I share or expose a precious part of myself. Like an artwork, a feeling, an idea I feel passionate about. Critic begins to jump up and down,

STOP! Don't do it!! We could be killed! Seriously, what are you thinking? This is way too dangerous.

GETTING TO KNOW YOUR CRITIC

WHAT DO THEY SOUND LIKE?

- You are probably the worst person who has ever existed.
- You will die alone in a hole.
- You're lazy. You lack imagination. You suck.

WHEN DO THEY COME TO THE SURFACE?

- When I put myself out there.
- When I'm not being very productive.
- When I rest or take time out.
- When I try something new or challenging.
- When I care about a situation.

GET TO KNOW YOUR CRITIC

WHAT KINDS OF THINGS DOES YOUR CRITIC SAY?

WHEN DOES YOUR CRITIC START GETTING LOUD?

HOW DO YOU FEEL WHEN THE CRITIC GETS LOUD?

HOW DO YOU RESPOND?

Reflect. Write. Draw.

Good mates with the critic
is this guy ↓

SHOULD MONSTER

You should be doing more!

You should be okay with this.

You should be better already!

You shouldn't be feeling what you are feeling.

You really should get over this already.

You should be a good Person.

DRAW YOUR SHOULD MONSTER

WHAT ARE THE SHOULDS YOUR MONSTER PUTS ON YOU?

IT'S OKAY

TO HAVE FLAWS

TO BE IMPERFECT

TO MAKE LOTS OF MISTAKES

TO LET YOURSELF + OTHERS DOWN

TO DO OR SAY THINGS YOU DIDN'T WANT TO DO

TO HAVE WEAKNESSES

TO DO NOTHING WHEN YOU WISHED YOU DID SOMETHING

IT'S OKAY...

FLY YOUR KITE OF IMPERFECTIONS, MISTAKES + FLAWS.

sometimes I say really silly things that I don't mean.

Sometimes I ignore people I love instead of telling them how I feel.

Sometimes I don't stand up for what I believe.

MAKE A LIST

(make a list of imperfections and practice telling yourself, 'it's okay' and 'I still love you')

WHICH IMPERFECTIONS OR FLAWS MIGHT

AlSO BE GIFTS ASSETS OR OPPORTUNITIES?

My harsh inner critic or judge can be both a strength and a weakness.

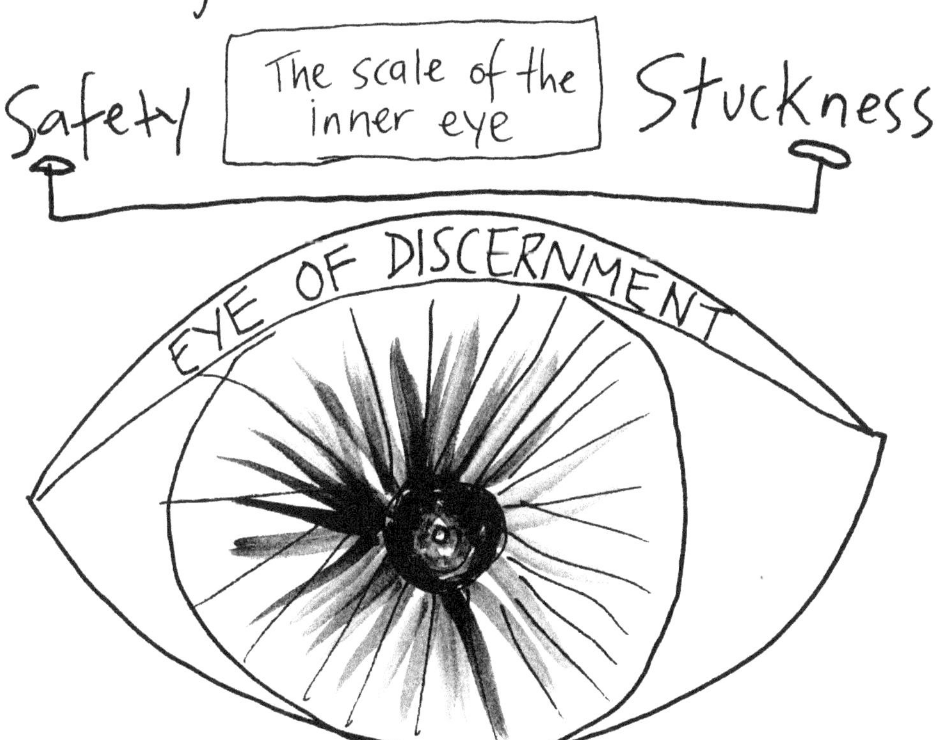

JUDGE

can be harsh + discouraging

can see beyond your optimism

can be discerning

judges situations or people as not OKAY

helps keep you safe

your child feels safe + secure

doesn't want to see you get hurt OR take risks

When is safe too safe?

prevents you from growing

IMPERFECTION. FLAW. WEAKNESS.

WHICH FLAWS MAY AlSO BE ASSETS?

GIFT. ASSET. STREGTH. OPPORTUNITY.

Tips for dealing with your critic

→ When you notice yourself in some kind of critical loop or shame spiral, write some of the judgements or criticisms on paper.

Then try reading them aloud in a silly voice
Even try singing them

♫ "I'm a really bad person yeah"

This helps to lessen their power. This technique is one I learnt from Russ Harris who is a practioner of Acceptance Commitment Therapy

Dialogue with your critic

Have a conversation with your critic and find out what they are really afraid of. It helps to do it on paper.

Listen + acknowledge their fears. Can you provide some support for the critic so they quieten down? How can you be kind to the critic? Or maybe you just accept that they are going to be critical and you move forward anyway.

"Thanks for sharing critic. I know you feel like we are going to get killed but finishing this book is really important to me."

Reflect. Write. Draw.

Reflect. Write. Draw.

feel

I have so many feelings

WORST! BEST! WHOOPS HEAVY HEART Love me HOPEFUL AM I EVEN ALIVE? REAL? AWAKE? COFFEE!

OUCH WHO ARE YOU? Blah! miss you WOOHOO I SUCK DAMN! LIKE

I just adore you ♡ Bliss EXCELENT CRIKEY! We Love Us! Meh YAH! RAGE! LOOK AT ME WHY? brilliance encapsulated

ALONE Confusion WHO THE #?*@ DO YOU THINK I AM? SUCCESS!! Joy SHITE CRAY I miss everyone...

That cat is whack MAD OVERWHELMED

TOUCH IT I'M TIRED I'm a whittle baby HELP! POOPY I AM SCARED. LOTS

I FEEL

- [ ] like a baby
- [ ] scared
- [ ] over it
- [ ] like I'm failing at life
- [ ] all alone
- [ ] the worst
- [ ] cray cray
- [ ] no one understands
- [ ] so sad
- [ ] everything is ruined
- [ ] overwhelmed
- [ ] like dying
- [ ] weirrrd
- [ ] fangry
- [ ] like a fraud
- [ ] waaaaaaa!
- [ ] impending doom
- [ ] all kinds of poo

I FEEL

- [ ] okay
- [ ] strong
- [ ] I am enough
- [ ] I'm killing it!
- [ ] All things considered I'm pretty great
- [ ] safe
- [ ] happy
- [ ] I'm doing the best I can.
- [ ] Filled with joy!
- [ ] Empowered
- [ ] grateful
- [ ] everything is okay
- [ ] brave
- [ ] luscious
- [ ] excited
- [ ] content
- [ ] YAY!
- [ ] lovely
- [ ] wise
- [ ] full of beans
- [ ] hopeful
- [ ] lucky!

today I notice...

if you like, put your hand on your heart and just allow yourself to feel what's going on. You don't need to like it, understand it, or even name it... Just allow yourself space to be exactly as you are...

WHAT CAN YOU FEEL?

What sensations are present in the body today?

What are the qualities, colour, texture, temperature of these sensations?

Are there any emotions attached to the sensations? Can you name them?

Any images, sounds, memories arising from the sensations?

BODY MAP (not to scale)

Peaceful

feels like a bright light shinning

spiky heat in neck

Some hard blocks

a wave through the neck

like some wire in elbow

warmth in the chest (heat + yellow glow)

slight tremble

hit of Churning

discomfort

anxiety/excitement

energy is the legs

Softness in the feet

BODY MAP (not to scale)

Make Your Own

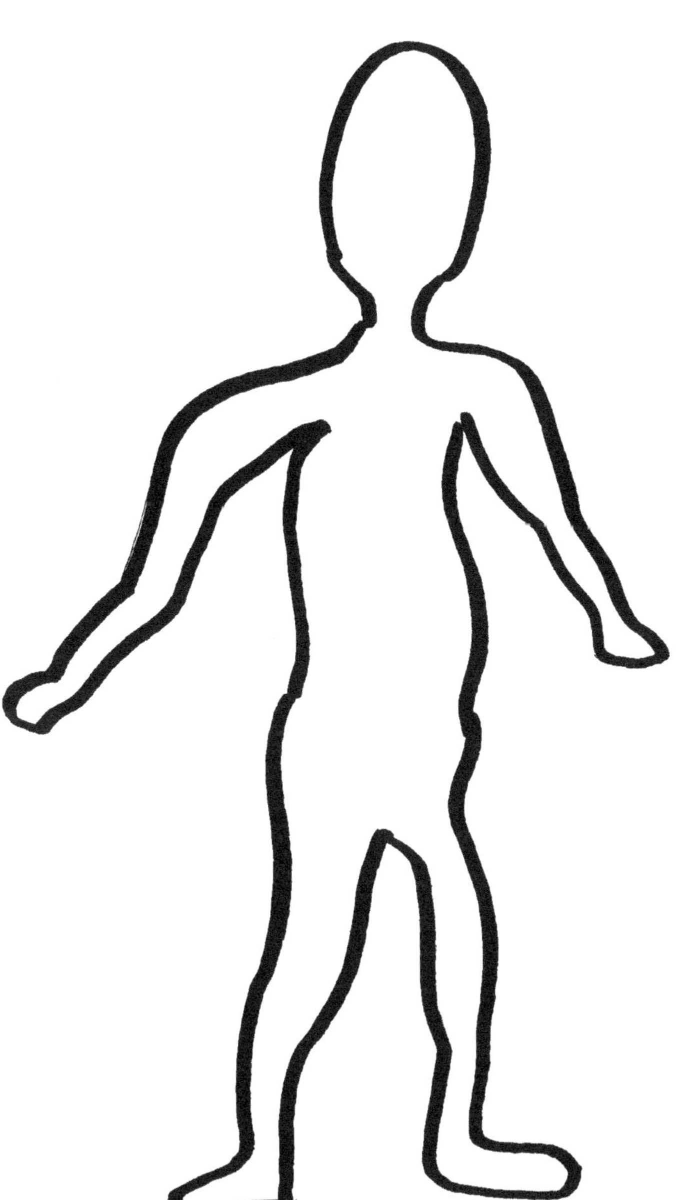

THANKS BODY!

Write or draw a message of gratitude to your body. Pay special attention to parts that need some extra tender loving kindness ü

MESSAGES OF KINDNESS TO YOUR BODY

today I accept
the imperfections
the tightness
the frustration
the fatigue
the pain
the sorrow

today I choose to
bring
kindness
patience
gentleness
acceptance
softness
to my body

FREE PLAY

FREE PLAY

rest

Practicing giving our bodies + beings deep rest is one of the best ways to feel compassion. Rest helps move our bodies from stress mode to relaxation and safety.

We are often so used to forcing and pushing ourselves to do and be more. Having a rest + allowing ourselves to stop can be uncomfortable. We may feel anxious and unsure of how to 'be' when we rest. Many of us will actively avoid rest because of the discomfort we feel. The discomfort we feel around rest is an opportunity to practice self-compassion. We can be kind to ourselves through rest + noticing what comes up when we rest.

GET UP!

GET GOING!

DO BE MORE BETTER DIFFERENT

WHAT IS YOUR RELATIONSHIP TO REST?

WHEN DID YOU LAST TAKE TIME OUT TO REST?

REST

HOW DO YOU REST + RELAX?

WHERE IN YOUR LIFE DO YOU PUSH YOURSELF?

Reflect. Write. Draw.

Reflect. Write. Draw.

REST CHALLENGE:

PLAN A COLLAPSE

NOT A HOLIDAY OR A HANGOVER. An intentional period of time where you rest.

Make time for uniterrupted rest and allow yourself to feel what's going on. I usually find I am much more tired than I even knew.

HOW? Create space + plan.

- ☆ Can be a long weekend, one day, even half a day can be really beneficial.
- ☆ Practice being Kind through rest.

So ... what do you do?

- ☆ allow yourself to be.
- ☆ don't force yourself to do anything at all.
- ☆ it's all good if you stay in bed all day :)
- ☆ notice thoughts arising about being a lazy sod and say

"it's okay I'm choosing to rest I'm choosing to be kind to my body + being by allowing some down time ..."

- ☆ notice what arises for you.

my judgement is around not doing enough (so how dare I rest!). Your judgement may be around ....

What Comes Up Resting

I find it hard to rest I feel too uncomfortable

If I rest I'll get really behind on life

It's not safe for me to rest

I don't deserve to rest

Rest is for the weak

If I rest I might never get up!

WHAT PREVENTS YOU FROM RESTING + TAKING TIME OUT?

WHAT KINDS OF THOUGHTS + JUDGEMENTS ARISE FOR YOU AROUND RESTING + NOT RESTING?

WHEN CAN YOU PLAN TO HAVE A COLLAPSE?

It could be from 8-4 on a Sunday

Schedule Your Collapse Day

DAY-
TIME-
SIGNATURE:

YES IT'S OKAY TO STAY IN BED ALL DAY

LET YOUR PHONE HAVE A REST TOO

YOU DON'T HAVE TO DO ANYTHING!

JUST REST + BE KIND

NO FORCING ALLOWED

THERE'S NOTHING
YOU HAVE TO DO
JUST REMEMBER

I LOVE YOU

FREE PLAY

FREE PLAY

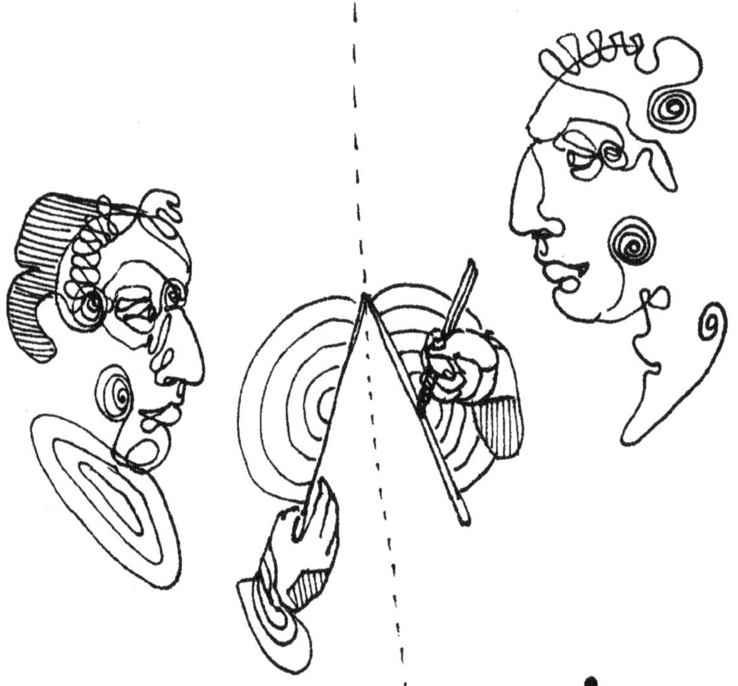

draw

Practice self-acceptance by becoming intimately acquainted with yourself.

- Take a selfie (just of your face)
- Sit and observe your face. Just look and notice the thoughts that arise.
- Practice being kind.

What thoughts arise when you look at your face . . .

You Are Beautiful

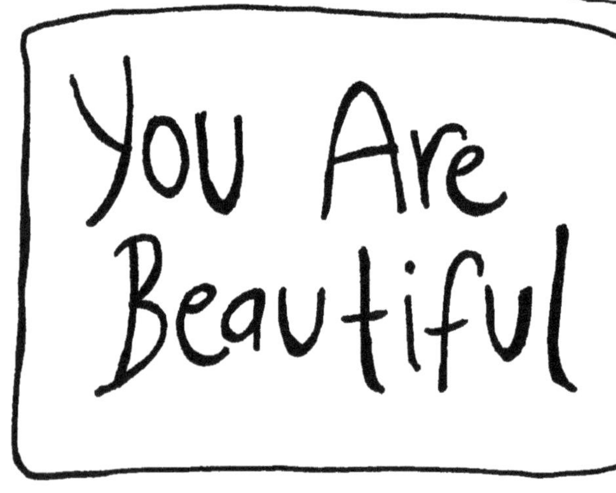

Practice some Kind Words

DRAW YOUR FACE

THINGS TO TRY

Semi Realistic

Cartoon

Minimal

Abstract

Dots or Tiny Strokes

Trippy

NOW TRY ANOTHER
(IN A DIFFERENT STYLE)

NOW TRY ANOTHER
(IN A DIFFERENT STYLE)

LIFE DRAWING

Accept imperfections in yourself + your drawing

If you notice yourself being harsh + critical

Practice being kind

Made mistake writing the word drawing (it's okay)

enjoy yourself and have fun!!

Full Body Drawing

Can be nude or clothed.
Take a photo or draw in front of a mirror.

Allow yourself to take in the entirety of your body. Start at the feet and just look and observe all the parts of you.

Then draw . . .

TRY DIFFERENT
POSITIONS

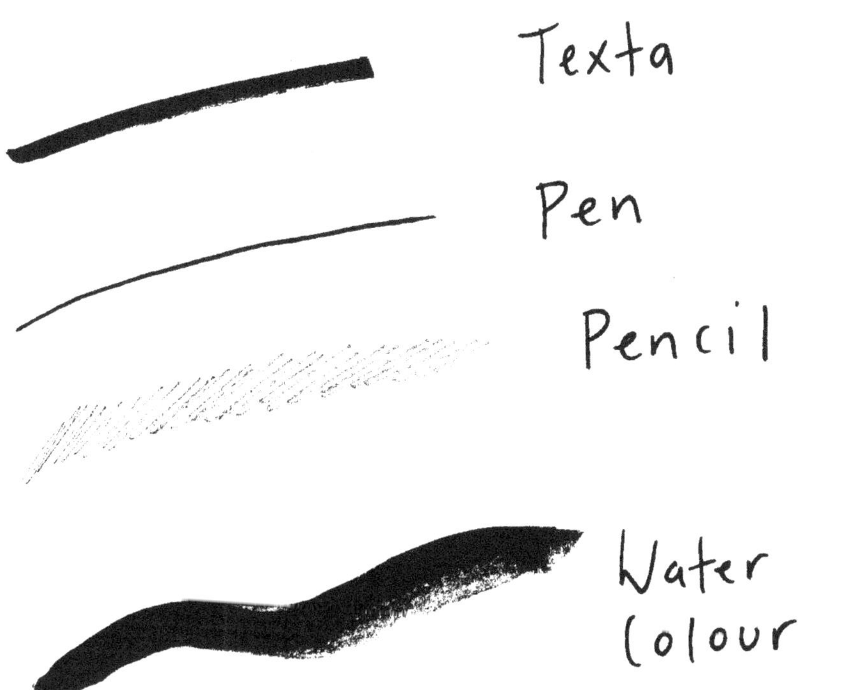

Try paint, Charcoal
Coloured pencils/crayons
Whatever you like

And Different
Styles

nourish

NOURISH

SLOW COOKING

- Set aside one night in the week to cook something special.
- Try something new, something you've been longing to try but haven4 had time.
- Clean up the kitchen and place all of the ingredients on the bench. Whisper a little blessing to the food.
- Begin the process with joy and excitement. Play your favourite music. Drink wine or tea. Take your time. Relish the process.
- When ready set the table. Light a candle. Give thanks to the food. Give thanks for nourishing yourself. Take time to taste, smell, chew + digest.

WATCHA GOT COOKING?

WHAT ARE
YOUR FAVOURITE
NOURISHING FOODS
+ DISHES?

ACTIVI-TEA

Take some time to make a delicious cup of tea, (even make it in a pot!), choose your favourite mug, make it slowly paying attention to the moment.

Find a nice spot in a garden or courtyard where you can feel comfortable and relaxed. Take your time to drink your precious cup of tea noticing how it feels in your mouth and body. Allow yourself to drink the tea and enjoy.

Homemade Pizza

Boy In The Bubble
Paul Simon

the scent of baked apple pie

warm coat on a windy day

Jacaranda Trees In Bloom

What are the images, memories, dreams desires, sounds and scents you associate with feeling nourished? (Write or Draw)

Nourish

SELECT A PIECE OF MUSIC
MOVE!
FIND YOURSELF A COMFORTABLE SPACE
HOW DOES MY BODY WANT TO MOVE?
ALLOW YOURSELF TO → DANCE JUMP, WRITHE, STRETH, ROLL WHATEVER YOU FEEL. DO IT!!!

WHAT'S YOUR JAM?

Music to move to. Write your playlist of favourite tracks

SONG NAME	ARTIST

WRITE DRAW DANCE SING BREATHE...

WHAT DO I NEED IN THIS MOMENT?

Throughout the course of your day practice asking yourself what you need and practice giving yourself a little kindness break. Dance to a favourite song. Get up and have a good stretch. Take some time out at lunch to journal or draw. Pick a flower for your bedroom. Take a few delicious deep breaths.

IDEAS FOR KINDNESS BREAKS

every hour I will stop to pat myself on the back

USE YOUR WORDS

Use your voice to nourish + support

* Write yourself a little prayer or affirmation or wish or spell or whatever you want to call it.
* Tap into friend within or a poet or song writer you admire for inspiration.
* Acknowledge, support + encourage yourself.
* Practice reading aloud with conviction.

THE FRIEND WITHIN

tap into this voice

what would your best friend say to you if you were battling?

YOU ARE DOING THE THINGS! KEEP GOING. I LOVE YOU ♡ YOU ARE ENOUGH. IT'S OKAY EVERYTHING IS IN ITS RIGHT PLACE. JUST KEEP SWIMMING!

We Love Us!

in your own words...

YOU DON'T NEED
TO FIND YOUR VOICE

YOU HAVE
A VOICE

YOU JUST NEED
TO PRACTICE
USING IT!

FREE PLAY

FREE PLAY

love

FORGIVE YO'SELF!

WHAT ARE YOU HOLDING ON TO?

STILL BEATING YOURSELF UP ABOUT?

IN A SHAME SPIRAL?

REALLY REGRET DOING OR NOT DOING?

FEEL SUPER GUILTY, YUCKY ICKY, MURKY, STICKY, STUCK?

BRING IT TO THE LOVE MOTHER!

ALL POWERFUL
LOVEMOTHER
IS SUPER DUPER
COMPASSIONATE

Imagine the most compassionate loving, understanding + comforting person you can think of...

Can be a real person

Someone fictional

Someone you create in your head

THEY ARE WISE LOVING KIND STRONG + COMPASSIONATE

DRAW THEM OR WRITE A DESCRIPTION OF THEM HERE

Imagine sitting down with the love mother by the fireside with a cup of tea. You are warm comfortable and safe.

Tell the love mother about something you've been beating yourself up about...

Imagine love mother listens without judgement and her kind smiling eyes receive whatever it is that you are telling her...

NOW imagine YOU are the LOVE MOTHER

WHAT DO YOU SAY TO YOURSELF?

I see you. I hear you. I love you. You were doing your best with the awareness you had at the time.

You couldn't have done anything differently. You don't need to torture yourself anymore. You have punished yourself enough. The time has come to put the stick down. I love you no matter what. You will grow and learn from this.

A letter to myself at age ______.

This is an oldie but a goodie. Choose a time in your life when you were battling pretty hard with being kind to yourself. (Could be years ago, or a month) Write to this self and channel the love mother and the friend within. Shower this past self with kindness, reassurance and compassion. Let them know you are here to help!

Letter to a past self

Letter to a past self

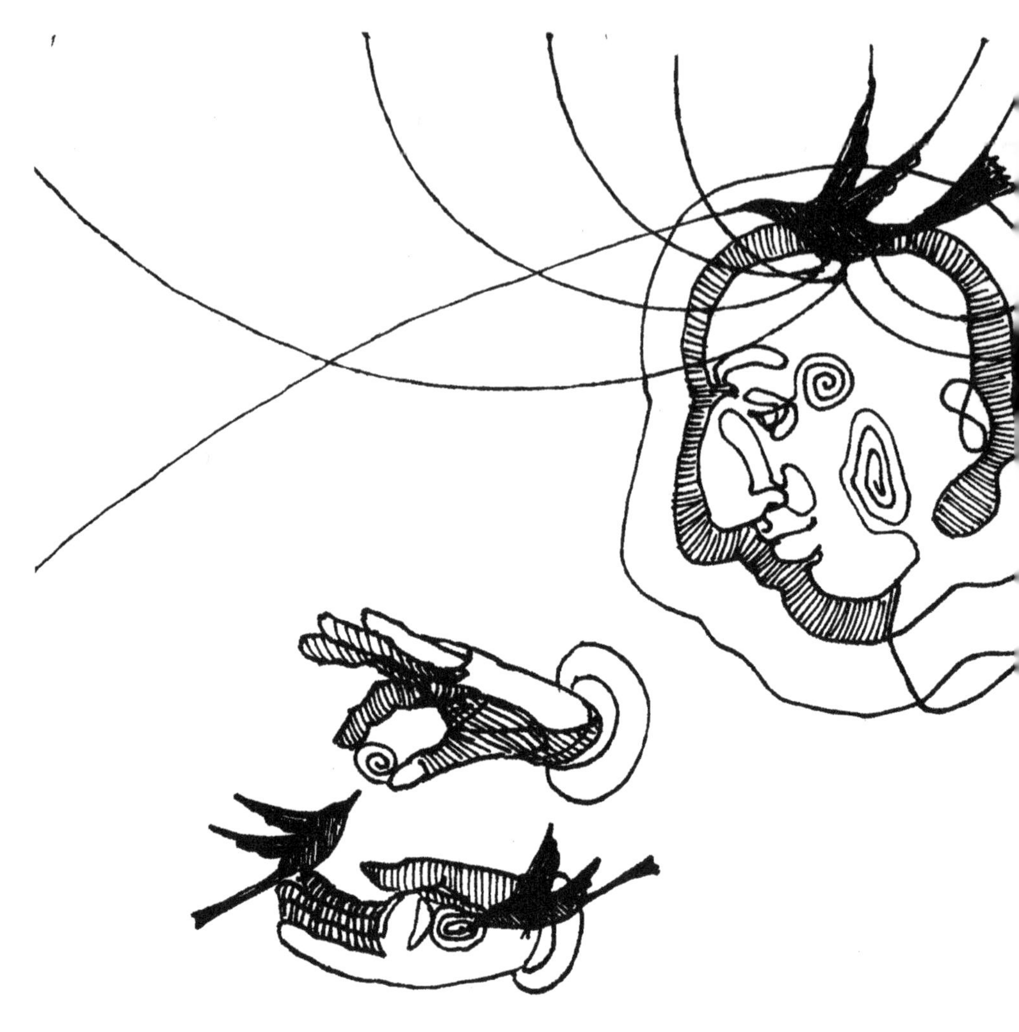

Support

TOUGH LOVE

Sometimes being kind requires boundaries, limits, self discipline and saying NO. Saying NO to situations, behaviours or relationships that are not okay for us.

We may need this to accomplish something important to us. Like study or a project.

Compassionate Boundaries

It may be something that feels hard + not so fun but has long term gains. Like exercise.

Making a habit or routine can make it easier with less struggle.

Your inner child may tantrum + cry. And really not want to keep doing the thing.

Rewarding yourself for keeping your commitments to yourself can help motivate you + the child.

Reflect

Where in your life could you apply compassionate boundaries?

think about something that's really important to you . . .

- finishing a project
- having a daily exercise routine
- practicing meditation
- doing some art or writing

WRITE OR DRAW IT HERE

COMMIT

COULD YOU COMMIT TO DOING IT REGULARLY?

(MAKE A COMMITMENT TO YOURSELF HERE).

REWARDS

How can you reward yourself?

(Brainstorm some daily, weekly + even long term rewards)

Rewards can be different from other self-care activities. They may be the same or similiar activity but they have the intention of celebration and acknowlegement at the forefront.

REWARDS

= nice thing + experienced intentionally + acknowledging the self for an accomplishment + celebration

YAY!

Your REWARD is watching any movie you like with a special treat like icecream or chocolate

We might watch a movie and eat ice cream any night of the week but when you make the experience a reward for your hardwork it can feel extra special.

Without actively acknowledging ourselves through kind words, pats on the back + special rewards we can get weighed down and unmotivated and even depressed.

Often this is when our kid will start tantruming and demanding treats + special treatment.

This is fair, given we have not been very kind to them.

However it's often when the kid reaches that level of dissatisfaction + upset that we can easily slip into self destructive behaviours (like binge eating, drinking + watching).

MAYBE THE KID (WHICH IS US) WOULD GET LESS NUTS + UPSET IF WE COULD BE CONSISTENTLY ACKNOWLEDGING OURSELVES + GIVING + RECEIVING REWARDS.

Rewards

Micro Rewards
Moments of
Self Acknowledgement

taking a long deep breathe

smiling

patting self on back

saying Well Done to our self + child self

WRITE ONE YOU CAN DO

Daily Rewards

WRITE SOME FOR YOURSELF

having a bubble bath

Watching doggo meme videos

Medium to Long Term Rewards

going on a trip

WRITE YOURS

PARTICIPATION AWARD

NAME:

AWARDED FOR:

FREE PLAY

FREE PLAY

heal

It's okay to feel (and not feel)

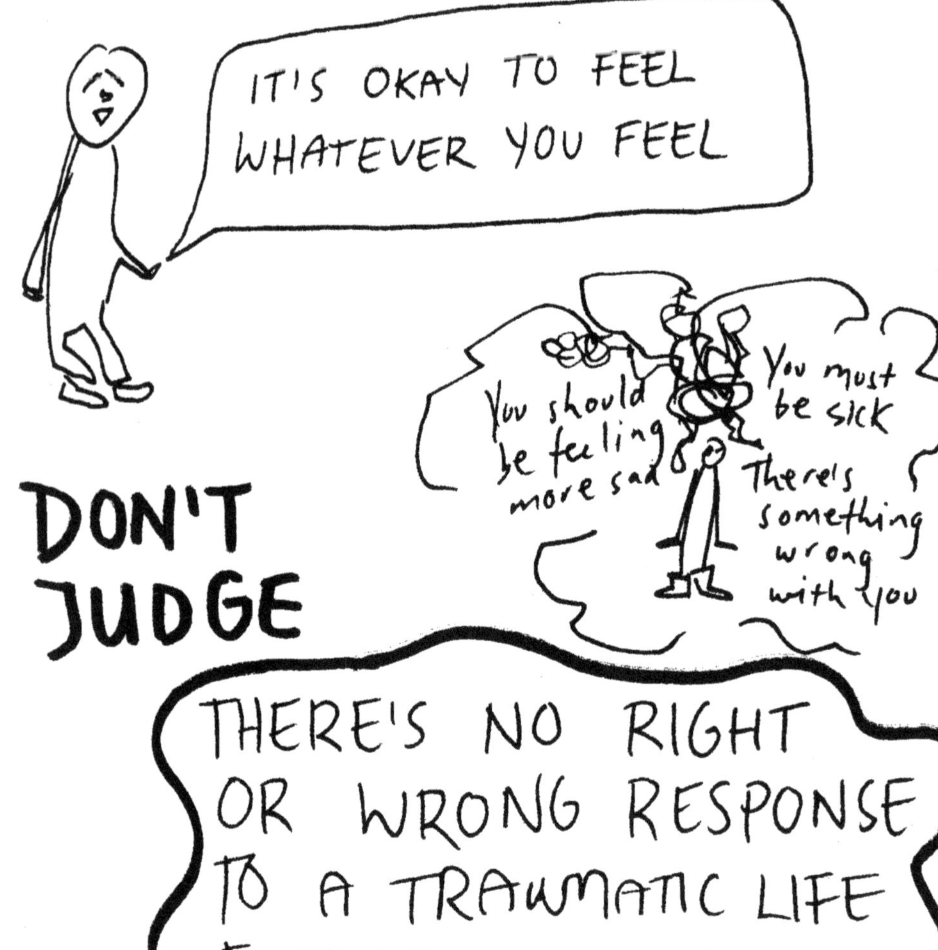
IT'S OKAY TO FEEL WHATEVER YOU FEEL
You should be feeling more sad
You must be sick
There's something wrong with you
DON'T JUDGE
THERE'S NO RIGHT OR WRONG RESPONSE TO A TRAUMATIC LIFE EVENT, OR ANY EVENT FOR THAT MATTER.

PRACTICE USING YOUR INTUITION

Listen.

Find a quiet spot. close your eyes. Ask a question

Go with what you receive. Take action.

Ask Yourself for guidance

TRUST THAT YOU KNOW WHAT YOU NEED.

BUILD A FORT

a magical land, where you can bring all the special things you need to sit + be.

What's in your fort? Draw · Write · Reflect

I WANT YOU
TO GROW BIG
+ STRONG

YOU ARE
DOING GREAT

I LOVE YOU

Sharing our pain + suffering helps us feel less alone.

We realise others have similiar struggles.

Practice reaching out to people when you need help + support.

CONNECT

I'm not alone

the light and love in me sees the light + love in you

SHARE

open to receive

open to give

100%

REACH OUT TREE

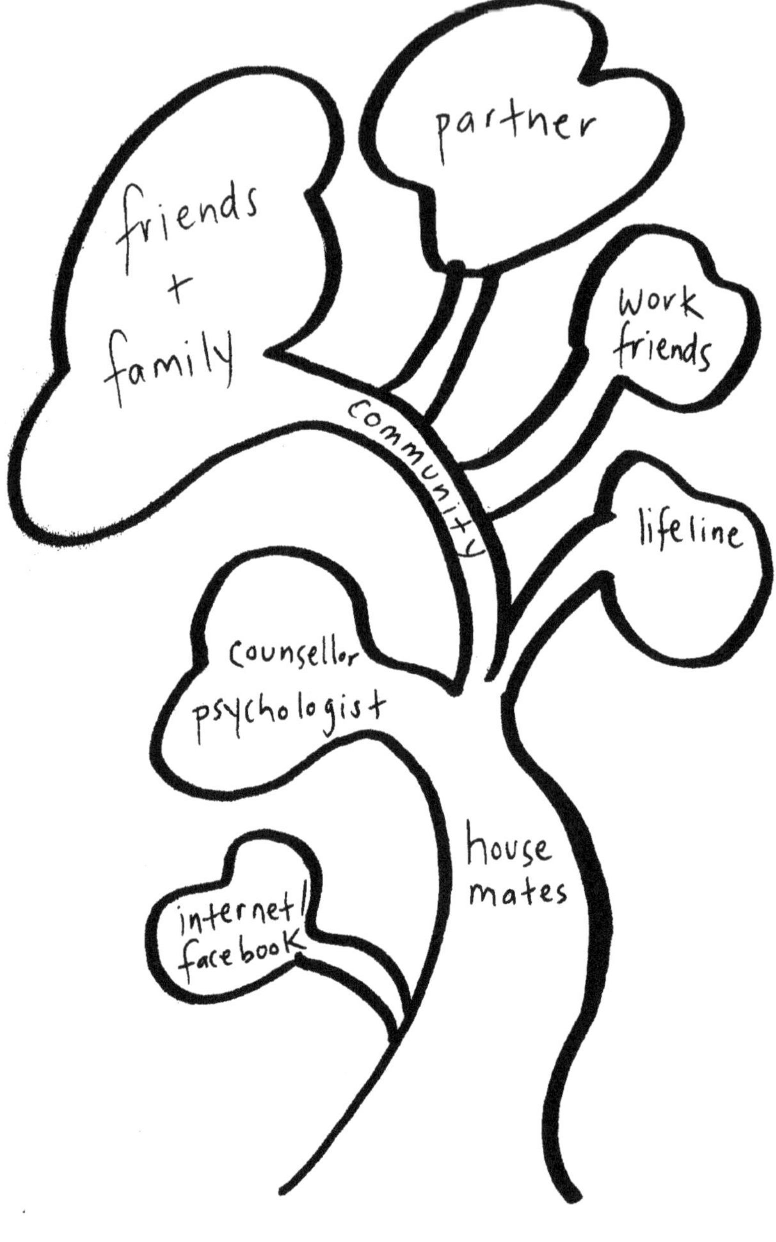

partner

friends
+
family

work
friends

community

lifeline

counsellor
psychologist

house
mates

internet/
facebook

WHO CAN YOU REACH OUT TO?

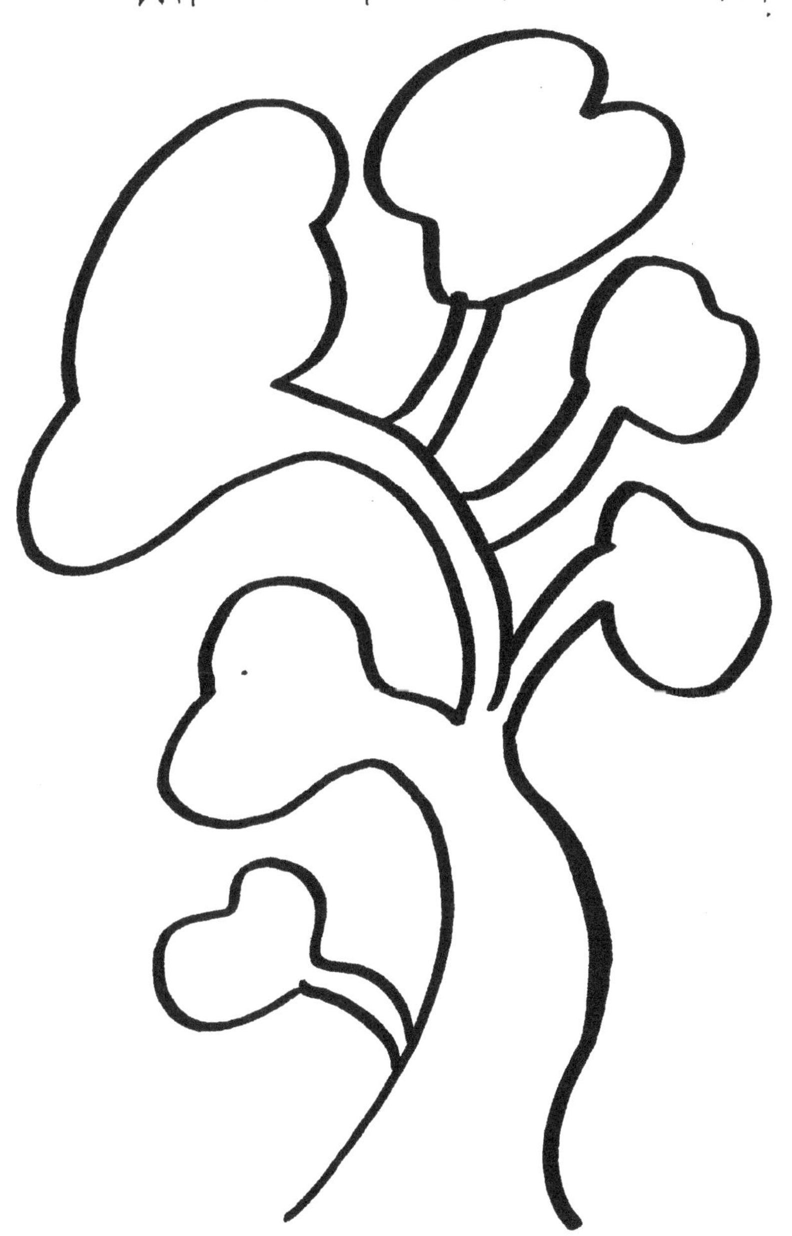

SELF-COMPASSION QUICK LIST

a go-to guide to being kind...

- grab a pen and paper & stream of consciousness write or draw.
- put on your favourite music, turn off the lights & dance yourself silly.
- get out into the backyard and pull out some weeds. get your hands dirty!
- breathe. to breathe deeper inhale counting to 5, hold the breath for 5, exhale for 5.
- solo mission into wild nature. If you can't get to the bush, a park or body of water is great too. walk & be outside.
- do some yoga, qi gong or tai chi (even for 20 minutes) look up a youtube video to guide you.
- read or listen to a book or story that's special.

- write a list of 20 things you are grateful for, remember all the good things.
- have a bath. make it really luscious experience with candles, bath salts, a glass of wine. After, moisturise your entire body & whisper kind words to it.
- go to water. immerse yourself. swim. splash around. or sit or walk by the waters edge. be refreshed + renewed.
- give yourself a gift! Seriously buy yourself something special that makes your heart sing (or your child really happy).
- Sing a song, and or read a poem aloud. Allow your voice to be heard (even if you are the only one listening.
- Look at the sky and watch the clouds passing by. Remember 'this too will pass'
- Get amongst some fire. Make a fire. Sit by the fire. Stare into the fire.
- Find a comfortable spot (without your phone), allow yourself to day dream, doodle, write or just be still.

WRITE YOUR OWN QUICK LIST HERE

THINK OF ALL YOUR FAVOURITE WAYS TO SHOW YOURSELF KINDNESS + LOVE.

FREE PLAY

Thanks

Thanks for buying this book, it supports my life + work which means making more things like this is possible.

Thanks to all my friends + family who have supported me in the process of writing this + supported my life + being.

Special thanks to Eleanor Coffey for your poetic contribution + to Jen Watkins for your chapter illustrations, love + constant encouragement. Big Love, Liz

About

Elizabeth is an artist, filmmaker + community arts facilitator. She has just started Space Whale. Space Whale provides creative services + resources to support well-being + creativity.

Elizabeth lives on the Central Coast, NSW, Australia.

She is passionate about using creativity to support well-being + transform lives.

Join The Community

Share your kindness + self-compassion journey...

Insta: @spacewhalearts
FB : @spacewhalearts
www.spacewhale.com.au

www.ingramcontent.com/pod-product-compliance
Ingram Content Group UK Ltd.
Pitfield, Milton Keynes, MK11 3LW, UK
UKHW062255290726
14090UKWH00017B/708